COSTA RICA T
GUIDE

G000111538

AMANDA .R. BRITT

Copyright

2023 Costa Rica Travel Guide. All rights reserved. No part of this publication may be reproduced, distributed, or transmitted in any form or by any means, including photocopying, recording, or other electronic or mechanical methods, without the prior written permission of the publisher. The information contained herein is provided for informational and educational purposes only, and is not intended to be a substitute for professional advice. Costa Rica Travel Guide does not accept any responsibility or liability for any decisions made or actions taken based on the information provided in this guide.

Table of Contents

Introduction

Conclusion

Introduction

Welcome to Costa Rica! This nation is recognized for its magnificent scenery, engaging culture, and rich animals. Whether you're hoping to relax in a seaside hammock, explore beautiful rainforests, or find hidden jewels, Costa Rica can provide you an amazing experience.

Costa Rica is a tiny Central American republic situated between Nicaragua and Panama. With a population of just under five million, Costa Rica is a tranquil country that has become an appealing destination for visitors from all over the globe. The country is recognized for its dedication to protecting its natural environment, and its efforts have earned it the status as one of the most environmentally friendly countries in the world.

Costa Rica is a bustling nation with an abundance of activities to satisfy every kind of tourist. From relaxing on the white sand beaches of the Caribbean or Pacific coasts, to volcano hikes and zip lining under the rainforest canopy, there is something for everyone. Costa Rica is also home to a variety of national parks, reserves, and animal refuges, making it a perfect destination for eco-tourists who wish to experience the country's amazing biodiversity.

Costa Rica has a rich culture that is represented in its unique cuisine, music, and rituals. From native specialities like gallo pinto (rice and beans), to traditional folk music, you may enjoy a genuine experience in Costa Rica. The nation is also recognized for its friendly residents, who are typically more than ready to share their traditions and tales with tourists.

Costa Rica is a safe and economical location for vacationers. The nation boasts a stable democracy, and a trustworthy infrastructure, making it a perfect area to visit. Costa Rica also provides a range of housing alternatives, from budget-friendly hostels and guesthouses, to luxury resorts and villas.

Whether you're searching for a peaceful beach holiday, an adventurous exploration of the country's unique biodiversity, or a cultural adventure to learn about Costa Rica's customs, this travel guide will help you make the most of your trip. From picking the right spot, to locating the greatest restaurants, to learning about the country's traditions and culture, this guide will give you all the knowledge you need to make your Costa Rica trip unique. So let's get started!

I. Planning Your Trip

A. When to Visit

Costa Rica is a wonderful place for holidaymakers and travelers alike. From its beautiful rainforests and breathtaking beaches to its bustling culture and dynamic towns, Costa Rica offers something for everyone. With its lush tropical rainforests, diversified animals, and breathtaking volcanic peaks, Costa Rica is a fantastic place for a fantasy trip. Whether you're seeking for an amazing adventure, a tranquil beach vacation, or a cultural experience, Costa Rica is sure to offer something for you. With that in mind, these are the ideal dates to visit Costa Rica for the ultimate holiday.

The dry season in Costa Rica normally extends from late November until late April. This is the most popular season to visit Costa Rica and the greatest time to enjoy the country's dry climate. Temperatures at this season are normally between 70 and 80 degrees Fahrenheit, giving it the ideal time to explore the country's plentiful animals, bask on its lovely beaches, or take in its lively culture.

Rainy season in Costa Rica extends from May to late November and is the least popular time to visit. While the rain may be strong this season, it is also the perfect time to explore the country's gorgeous jungles and rich animals. Temperatures at this period are normally between 70 and 90 degrees Fahrenheit. However, it is crucial to know that certain of the country's roads and attractions might be difficult to reach during this season owing to the rain.

For those seeking an eco-friendly holiday, Costa Rica provides some of the greatest options for eco-tourism in the world. With its plentiful fauna and breathtaking scenery, it is the ideal location for eco-friendly vacationers. The greatest time to visit Costa Rica for an eco-friendly holiday is from late December to mid-April. This is when the nation is at its driest, making it simpler to explore its beautiful jungles and abundant fauna. Additionally, at this season the climates are milder and the days are longer, enabling guests to make the most of their stay in Costa Rica.

If you're hoping to experience the culture of Costa Rica, the ideal time to come is around the Christmas and New Year's holidays. During this season, the country comes alive with festivities and celebrations. From the historic "Día de Los Reyes" in December to the bright "Fiestas de la Cruz" in April, there is something for everyone to enjoy. Additionally, at this period the country's cities come alive with music, dancing, and art.

No matter when you choose to visit Costa Rica, you're guaranteed to experience the vacation of a lifetime. With its beautiful jungles, breathtaking beaches, rich culture, and plentiful animals, Costa Rica is the ideal destination for every tourist. Whether you're seeking an eco-friendly adventure, a peaceful beach escape, or a cultural experience, Costa Rica is guaranteed to deliver the right holiday for you.

B. Visa Requirements

One of the most beautiful and varied nations in Central America, Costa Rica offers a plethora of natural and cultural attractions. To enter this nation, travelers must fulfill the visa requirements of Costa Rica. Depending on the purpose of their visit and their nationality, tourists may need to get a visa before their journey or upon arrival.

Tourist Visa

Foreign nationals from most countries, including the US, are eligible to travel to Costa Rica without a visa for up to 90 days. Upon arrival, travelers must produce a valid passport, as well as evidence of adequate means to maintain themselves while in the nation. In rare situations, passengers may additionally be requested to present evidence of an onward or return ticket. In addition, visitors may be requested to present evidence of medical insurance in case of an emergency.

Business Visa

Foreign people who intend to go to Costa Rica for business reasons must get a business visa. This visa is valid for up to 90 days and may be renewed for an additional 90 days. To apply for a business visa, candidates must provide a valid passport and give documentation that they are employed or have an invitation from a Costa Rican firm.

Student Visa

Foreign individuals who intend to study in Costa Rica must get a student visa. This visa is valid for up to one year and may be extended upon request. To apply for a student visa, candidates must present a valid passport, a copy of their admission letter from a Costa Rican institution, evidence of adequate finances to maintain themselves while in the country, and proof of medical insurance.

Work Visa

Foreign citizens who wish to work in Costa Rica must obtain a work visa. This visa is valid for up to one year and may be extended upon request. To apply for a work visa, candidates must present a valid passport, evidence of employment from a Costa Rican employer, proof of adequate means to maintain themselves while in the country, and proof of medical insurance.

Residency Visa

Foreign nationals who intend to live in Costa Rica for a lengthy period of time must get a resident visa. This visa is valid for up to one year and may be extended upon request. To apply for a resident visa, candidates must present a valid passport, evidence of work or sufficient finances to sustain themselves while in the nation, and proof of medical insurance.

Transit Visa

Foreign individuals who need to pass through Costa Rica must get a transit visa. This visa is valid for up to 48 hours and cannot be extended. To apply for a transit visa, applicants must produce a valid passport, evidence of an onward or return ticket, and proof of medical insurance.

In conclusion, tourists must fulfill the visa requirements of Costa Rica before entering the country. Depending on the purpose of their visit, tourists may need to get a tourist visa, business visa, student visa, work visa, residence visa, or transit visa ahead of their journey. It is essential to note that the visa requirements for Costa Rica may change at any moment, so tourists should check with their local embassy or consulate for the most up-to-date information.

C. Safety Rules

Costa Rica is a lovely and dynamic nation with a rich and colorful culture. It is a popular location for visitors from throughout the globe, and with good reason. However, it is crucial to keep safety in mind while going to Costa Rica. Here are some safety guidelines to bear in mind when visiting Costa Rica.

1. Be aware of your surroundings at all times. While Costa Rica is a generally secure place, it is vital to remain alert of your surroundings and the people around you. Be cautious to remain in well-lit, busy locations and avoid wandering alone at night. You should also be careful of pickpockets and other small crimes.

2. Do not leave valuables in public spaces. Pickpockets and other crooks may be searching for an opportunity to take your valuables. Do not leave important things, such as wallets, handbags, or jewelry, in plain sight in public settings.

3. Use caution while interacting with strangers. Costa Rica is typically a secure area, however it is vital to remain careful while interacting with strangers. Be wary of any strange behavior, and if you feel uneasy, it is advisable to leave the area.

4. Be aware of local laws. While Costa Rica is usually a safe location, there are specific rules and regulations that tourists must respect. Be cautious to check the local regulations before visiting, and be aware of any limitations in place.

5. Avoid illicit narcotics. The possession, distribution, or sale of illicit narcotics is strongly forbidden in Costa Rica. If detected, you may be liable to harsh penalties, including prison time.

6. Keep your passport and other papers secure. It is crucial to maintain your passport and other critical papers safe and secure at all times. Never leave them in a public location, or leave them in your hotel room unattended.

7. Follow traffic laws. Driving in Costa Rica may be a difficulty, and it is necessary to respect all local traffic restrictions. Be careful to wear a seatbelt at all times, and respect all traffic signals and signs.

8. Use caution while swimming in the ocean. Be mindful of the water's conditions, and take care while swimming in the ocean. Be mindful to remain in shallow seas and away from rip currents.

9. Be aware of natural disasters. Costa Rica is subject to natural calamities, such as floods and earthquakes. Be cautious to investigate the local weather conditions before visiting, and be aware of any cautions or alerts issued by the local authorities.

10. Have a travel plan. Before going, make sure to have a plan in place in case of an emergency. Have a contact list of relatives and friends, and know the contact details of the local embassy or consulate.

Following these safety tips when going to Costa Rica may assist guarantee a safe and pleasurable vacation. Be careful to keep aware of your surroundings, and take caution while engaging with strangers. Be mindful of local rules and regulations, and always keep your passport and other papers secure. Use care while swimming in the water, and be alert of natural calamities. Lastly, have a travel plan in place in case of an emergency. By following these safety regulations, you may assure a safe and happy vacation to Costa Rica.

D. GettingAround.

Costa Rica is a tiny Central American republic situated between Nicaragua and Panama. With its lush jungles, stunning beaches, and abundant wildlife, Costa Rica is one of the most popular tourist destinations in the world. Getting about Costa Rica is pretty straightforward and there are several transportation alternatives that may be utilized to tour the nation.

The most common method to move about Costa Rica is through hiring a vehicle. Car rental firms are accessible across the nation and provide both manual and automatic cars. The most common kind of automobile to hire in Costa Rica is a 4x4, since the roads may be very hard in certain locations. It is vital to know that Costa Rica does not need an international driver's license, but it is advised for safety.

Taxis are another popular method to move about Costa Rica. Taxis are easily accessible in most big cities and towns and may be called from the street. However, it is crucial to understand that taxis in Costa Rica are not metered, therefore it is vital to agree on a fee before getting into the cab. It is also worth mentioning that bargaining is a prevalent habit in Costa Rica, so it is wise to discuss the price of the cab before getting in.

Public transit is also accessible in Costa Rica, albeit it is not as dependable as in other nations. Buses are the most frequent mode of public transportation in Costa Rica, and they are accessible to most major cities and communities. Buses may be hailed from the side of the road, and they are relatively reasonable.

Traveling by boat is also an option in Costa Rica. There are multiple ferry services that travel between the Caribbean and Pacific coastlines, as well as smaller boats that run between different towns and cities. These boats may be a terrific way to visit the many sections of Costa Rica, and they are quite reasonable.

Finally, it is also feasible to go about Costa Rica by aircraft. There are numerous large airports around the nation, and domestic flights are accessible to most major cities and villages. Flying is the quickest and most convenient method to get across Costa Rica, albeit it may be fairly pricey.

Overall, traveling about Costa Rica is quite straightforward, and there are various transportation alternatives accessible. Renting a vehicle is the most common method to move about Costa Rica, while taxis, public transit, ferries, and airlines are all available. It is crucial to understand that bargaining is a frequent habit in Costa Rica, so it is recommended to discuss pricing before getting into a cab or riding a boat.

E. Where to Stay

Costa Rica is a gorgeous, tropical nation situated in Central America that features spectacular vistas of the Caribbean Sea, Pacific Ocean, and thick jungles. With its magnificent beaches, wonderful wildlife, and distinct culture, Costa Rica is a popular destination for travelers from all over the globe. Whether you're searching for a deluxe hotel or a more budget-friendly choice, here are some of the greatest places to stay in Costa Rica.

If you're searching for a lavish stay, there are a choice of resorts and hotels around Costa Rica. For those searching for an all-inclusive vacation, the Occidental Papagayo Resort & Spa is a terrific option. Situated on the Pacific Coast, this resort provides breathtaking views of the ocean, as well as an infinity pool and a private beach. The resort also provides a range of activities, such as snorkeling and zip-lining, as well as wonderful restaurants and bars.

For a more budget-friendly stay, there are dozens of hostels and guesthouses across Costa Rica. Hostels are an excellent alternative for travelers and people wishing to meet other travelers. Hostel Pangea in the city of San Jose, for example, provides cheap dormitory-style accommodations as well as individual rooms for a more pleasant stay. There are also a variety of guesthouses located throughout the country, such as the Casa del Sol in the city of Monteverde, which offers comfortable and affordable accommodations with a unique, homey atmosphere.

If you're looking for a truly unique experience, Costa Rica also offers a variety of eco-lodges. These lodges are situated in the middle of the rainforest and provide guests with an unforgettable experience. They often feature a variety of activities, such as guided hikes and bird-watching, as well as delicious, locally-sourced meals. The Pacuare Lodge, for example, is a luxurious eco-lodge located along the Pacuare River that provides an unforgettable experience.

Finally, if you're looking for something a bit more off-the-beaten-path, Costa Rica also has a variety of camping sites. These sites are often situated in remote areas of the country, offering guests a chance to explore the beauty of the rainforest. The Lapa Rios Ecolodge, for example, offers a variety of camping sites in the Osa Peninsula. These sites offer breathtaking views of the ocean, as well as access to a variety of activities such as kayaking and bird-watching.

No matter what your budget or preferences, there is something for everyone in Costa Rica. From luxurious resorts and eco-lodges to budget-friendly hostels and camping sites, there are plenty of options for an unforgettable stay in Costa Rica. So, the next time you're planning a trip to Costa Rica, be sure to check out the variety of accommodations available to find the perfect place to stay.

II. Exploring Costa Rica

A. Tourist Attractions

Costa Rica is one of the most scenic and attractive nations in the world. With its lush tropical forests, lovely beaches, and unusual fauna, Costa Rica is a popular destination for travelers. From the zipline over the rainforest canopy to touring its several national parks, there is something for everyone in Costa Rica. Here are just a handful of the top tourist sites in Costa Rica that you don't want to miss.

The Arenal Volcano is one of the most recognizable sites in Costa Rica. Located in the northern province of Alajuela, this active volcano is one of the most visited sites in the country. Visitors may take a guided tour of the volcano or trek up to its top for stunning views. The surrounding area is also home to a variety of hot springs and waterfalls, making it a perfect spot to rest and take in the natural beauty of the region.

Another popular attraction for travelers is the Manuel Antonio National Park. Located on the Pacific coast near the city of Quepos, this park is famed for its white-sand beaches, lush vegetation, and rich fauna. Here, tourists may explore the paths, discover monkeys, sloths, and a variety of other species, and take a plunge in the warm waters of the neighboring Playa Espadilla.

If you're seeking for a unique experience, then a visit to the Monteverde Cloud Forest Reserve is a must. Located in the northern province of Puntarenas, this reserve is noted for its outstanding biodiversity and stunning panoramas. Here, tourists may discover the unique flora and wildlife of the area and take part in a range of outdoor activities such as canopy tours, horseback riding, and zip lines.

Costa Rica is also home to a variety of stunning beaches. In the northern region of the nation, the popular beaches of Tamarindo, Playa Conchal, and Playa Flamingo offer a range of sports such as snorkeling, surfing, and stand-up paddle boarding. Further south, the beaches of Manuel Antonio, Dominical, and Uvita are particularly popular with holidaymakers. Whether you're searching for a calm area to rest or an action-packed beach day, Costa Rica offers it all.

Finally, no vacation to Costa Rica would be complete without seeing one of the country's numerous national parks. From the Arenal Volcano National Park to Corcovado National Park, there are a multitude of parks to visit. Here you may discover breathtaking scenery, rich animals, and lots of chances for outdoor activities like hiking, bird watching, and wildlife spotting.

Costa Rica is a terrific place for individuals seeking a unique and enjoyable holiday. With its gorgeous scenery, diversified animals, and countless activities, there is something for everyone in this lovely and distinct nation. From zip lining beneath the forest canopy to resting on the beach, Costa Rica is a location that you won't want to miss.

B. Outdoor Activities

When you think about Costa Rica, pictures of verdant rainforests, towering volcanoes, and gorgeous beaches spring to mind. But Costa Rica is much more than simply its natural beauty. It is a nation full of adventure, and there are lots of outdoor things to enjoy. From hiking and rafting to zip-lining and surfing, Costa Rica has something for everyone.

For those searching for a little adventure, Costa Rica offers some of the greatest hiking and trekking in Latin America. The country's hilly landscape affords lots of opportunity for exploration. Whether you're searching for a hard trip or a picturesque walk, there's something for everyone. Popular paths in Costa Rica include the Arenal Volcano National Park, the Rincon de la Vieja

National Park, and the Monteverde Cloud Forest Reserve. If you're searching for a more strenuous walk, you may try the Chirripo National Park or the Santa Elena Cloud Forest Reserve.

If you're looking for something a little more relaxed, Costa Rica is also home to some of the greatest beaches in the world. The country's Pacific and Caribbean shores provide lots of possibilities for sunbathing, swimming, and beachcombing. Popular beaches include Manuel Antonio National Park and Playa Hermosa. For a more isolated beach experience, try visiting the Isla del Coco or the Bahia Drake.

For those searching for an adrenaline rush, Costa Rica is the ideal spot for rafting, kayaking, and zip-lining. The country's rivers provide some of the greatest whitewater rafting in Latin America. Popular rafting companies include Desafio Adventure Company and Rios Tropicales. Kayakers can explore the country's magnificent alpine lakes and lagoons. The Arenal Volcano National Park and the Rincon de la Vieja National Park provide some of the greatest kayaking in Costa Rica. For a truly unique experience, zip-liners can soar through the jungle canopy and experience the beauty of Costa Rica's rainforest from a bird's eye view.

Surfing is another popular recreation in Costa Rica. The country's Pacific and Caribbean beaches provide lots of opportunity for surfers of all ability levels. Popular places include Tamarindo, Puerto Viejo, and Playa Hermosa. For a more private surfing experience, try visiting the Isla del Coco or the Bahia Drake.

Costa Rica is also home to some of the greatest wildlife watching possibilities in Latin America. The country is home to around 500 kinds of birds and hundreds of types of flora and animals. Popular wildlife-viewing areas include Corcovado National Park, Monteverde Cloud Forest Reserve, and the Tortuguero National Park.

No matter what outdoor activities you're searching for, Costa Rica provides something for everyone. From hiking and rafting to surfing and animal watching, the nation provides lots of options for adventure. So if you're seeking a unique outdoor experience, Costa Rica is the right place.

C. Cultural Experiences

Costa Rica is a nation that is rich with cultural experiences. Its colorful culture and breathtaking scenery make it a favorite destination for vacationers. From its colonial architecture and active arts scene to its magnificent beaches and jungles, Costa Rica offers a wealth of cultural activities.

The first thing to do while visiting Costa Rica is to discover the culture. From the main city of San Jose to the smaller towns and villages, each is rich with its own distinct combination of culture and history. Tourists may explore the colonial buildings, visit museums, and engage in traditional dances, music, and festivals.

Costa Rica is home to several diverse indigenous civilizations. These civilizations may be studied via the numerous various museums and archaeological sites around the nation. One of the most popular museums is the Pre-Columbian Gold Museum in San Jose, which shows ancient treasures from the ancient Chorotega and Diquis civilizations.

The nation is also host to several festivals and festivities throughout the year. In San Jose, the National Fiesta is held every year in April. This celebration features parades, live music, dancing, and street food. Other celebrations include the Semana Santa festival in Limon, the Carnaval de Limon, and many more.

Costa Rica also features a strong artistic culture. From the bright murals in San Jose to the many galleries around the nation, it is simple to find something to appreciate. In San Jose, the National Art Museum shows works by local and international artists. The National Theater is also a terrific venue to explore the culture, with shows ranging from ballet to opera.

Another approach to appreciate the culture of Costa Rica is to enjoy its beautiful natural beauty. The nation is home to some of the most gorgeous jungles in the world, with varied animals and fantastic climbs. A journey to the Monteverde Cloud Forest Reserve is a must-do, with its tremendous biodiversity and spectacular vistas. The Arenal Volcano National Park is also a popular location, with its hot springs and volcanic activity.

Finally, the nation features some of the most magnificent beaches in the world. From the white sand beaches of Guanacaste to the black sand beaches of Puerto Viejo, there is something for everyone. Whether you're searching for a lavish beach retreat or a more rustic experience, Costa Rica offers it all.

Costa Rica is a nation rich with culture, beauty, and adventure. From its magnificent beaches to its lively arts scene, there are so many cultural opportunities to be explored. Whether you're wanting to explore the jungle or enjoy the festivals and festivities, Costa Rica is guaranteed to give a one-of-a-kind experience.

D. Modes of Communication

Costa Rica is a tiny and lovely nation situated in Central America, with a population of almost four million people. It is recognized for its beautiful tropical rainforest, magnificent beaches, and abundant wildlife. It is also noted for its rich culture, friendly population, and robust economy. With so much to offer, it is no wonder that communication in Costa Rica is a fundamental component of daily life.

Costa Rica's principal language is Spanish, while some of the indigenous communities still retain their own language. English is also frequently spoken in various sections of the nation, notably in tourism regions. Most Costa Rican companies and government agencies speak Spanish, thus it is vital for expatriates and tourists to acquire some basic Spanish.

The major mediums of communication in Costa Rica are spoken, written, and digital. Verbal communication involves conversing face-to-face, on the phone, or on the radio. Written communication includes letters, emails, and text messages. Digital communication is generally done via the internet and social media, such as Facebook and Twitter.

Verbal communication is still the most preferred way of communication in Costa Rica. People prefer to speak in Spanish, however English is becoming more common due to tourism and the rising number of expatriates. Costa Ricans are exceedingly kind and are recognized for their eagerness to assist people in need. They are also quite open to cultural differences and are prepared to adapt to the language and habits of the person they are interacting with.

Written communication is also popular in Costa Rica. Letters, emails, and text messages are all used to communicate. There are post offices in most cities and villages, where individuals may send and receive mail.

Email is also common, with most companies and government organizations having email accounts. Text messages are getting more and more prevalent, since more individuals possess mobile phones.

Digital communication is becoming more common, as more individuals possess computers and have access to the internet. Social media is growing more popular, with the majority of Costa Ricans having at least one account on Facebook or Twitter. The internet is also used to access news, information, and services, such as banking and shopping.

Overall, communication in Costa Rica is largely done orally, with written and digital communication becoming more common. The predominant language is Spanish, however English is becoming more and more prevalent owing to tourists and expats. Costa Ricans are highly kind and receptive to cultural differences, and are eager to assist those in need. Written and digital communication are also prevalent, with email, text messaging, and social media growing more popular. As technology progresses, communication in Costa Rica will become even more easy and efficient.

III. Tips for a Memorable Trip

A. Eating Well

Eating healthily in Costa Rica is a terrific way to explore the local culture and food. Costa Rica is a nation famed for its bright tastes and various ingredients, and its cuisine is largely influenced by its location in Central America. With its lush jungles, rich fish, and tropical fruits, there are lots of alternatives for eating healthy in Costa Rica.

The first thing to remember while eating healthily in Costa Rica is that rice and beans constitute the backbone of the native cuisine. Rice and beans are frequently served with a side of plantains and a variety of other vegetables. This combination creates a healthy, full supper that is low in fat and calories. Plantains are a mainstay in Costa Rican cookery, and may be fried or boiled and eaten with savory sauces or sweet fruits.

Seafood is also quite popular in Costa Rica, and there are various recipes including fish, shrimp, and squid. The local fish markets provide a variety of fresh catches, and many restaurants serve traditional meals like fish and rice or ceviche.

Fruits are commonly accessible throughout Costa Rica, and they make a terrific snack or dessert. Tropical fruits such as mangoes, papayas, bananas, and pineapples are abundantly accessible and make a terrific complement to any meal. Fruits are frequently served as a side dish or combined into smoothies.

Vegetables are also an important part of eating well in Costa Rica. Vegetables such as tomatoes, bell peppers, squash, onions, and garlic are cooked in a number of ways, including sautéed, grilled, or boiled. Many vegetables are also used to prepare sauces and salsas, which are eaten with most meals.

Eating out in Costa Rica is also a terrific opportunity to enjoy the local food. Traditional Costa Rican restaurants provide foods such as grilled chicken and pig, paired with beans, rice, and plantains. Street food is also popular, with tamales, empanadas, and tacos being some of the most popular products.

Finally, Costa Rica is recognized for its coffee, and there are numerous cafés and restaurants that sell a range of specialty coffees and espresso cocktails. Coffee is an integral element of Costa Rican culture, and it is a terrific way to conclude a dinner or have a mid-afternoon pick-me-up.

Eating healthily in Costa Rica is a terrific way to discover the local culture and food. Whether you're searching for real street cuisine, traditional recipes, or a cup of coffee, Costa Rica has something to offer everyone. With its various ingredients and rich tastes, Costa Rica is the ideal place for a tasty, nutritious lunch.

B. Shopping Tips

Shopping in Costa Rica is an exciting and gratifying experience. Whether you are seeking souvenirs, local handicrafts, or simply a few things to take home with you, there are lots of alternatives. Here are some ideas to make your shopping excursion successful.

1. Know Where to Shop

Costa Rica offers a range of stores to pick from. In major cities like San Jose, you'll find typical department shops, shopping malls, and marketplaces. In smaller towns and villages, you'll discover artisan markets, local boutiques, and art galleries.

2. Know When to Shop

Costa Rican businesses and marketplaces tend to shut early (about 6 PM) (around 6 PM). Many shops are closed on Sunday, and some may also be closed on Monday. Before you plan your shopping excursion, carefully verify the opening and closing hours of the businesses you intend to visit.

3. Know What to Buy

Costa Rica is famed for its coffee, chocolate, and handicrafts. Coffee and chocolate are both high-quality and inexpensive. Handicrafts are a terrific way to take home a bit of Costa Rican culture. Popular goods include wood carvings, jewelry, and ceramics.

4. Be Prepared to Bargain

In many shops and marketplaces, it's normal to haggle over pricing. Don't be afraid to ask for a discount or negotiate a better price. It's also crucial to understand that certain shops may be ready to take US dollars or credit cards, but it's wise to come prepared with some Costa Rican colones.

5. Know Your Rights

It's crucial to be informed of your rights while buying in Costa Rica. Make sure to ask for a receipt for any transactions you make. If you have an issue with a purchase, you have the right to return it within 15 days.

6. Be Prepared for the Weather

Costa Rica's tropical climate may be unpredictable. Be sure to have an umbrella or raincoat with you while shopping, just in case it rains. The sun may be harsh, so don't forget to bring a hat and sunscreen, too.

7. Be Patient

Costa Rica is a laid-back nation, and the same applies for shopping. Don't be shocked if it takes a while for sellers to locate what you're searching for or if it takes longer than anticipated to complete a transaction. Be patient and don't hurry the procedure.

Shopping in Costa Rica is a joyful and rewarding activity. With a little planning, you can make the most of your shopping trip and select the right mementos to take home with you.

Conclusion

Costa Rica is an incredible place that should be on everyone's vacation list. It is a land of beautiful scenery, kind people, diverse cultures, and wonderful experiences. From the beaches of the Pacific and Caribbean coastlines to the stunning mountains and volcanoes, to the lush jungles and jungle fauna, Costa Rica has something for everyone.

No matter your age, money, or hobbies, there is something for every tourist in Costa Rica. Whether you're searching for a weekend break, an adventure-filled holiday, or a tranquil beach retreat, you'll find it in Costa Rica. With its natural beauty, friendly people, and different cultures, this is an excellent destination for every tourist.

The greatest way to enjoy Costa Rica is to stray off the main route and explore the country for yourself. While seeing the big tourist locations and attractions is fantastic, it's the small things that make Costa Rica distinctive. From the local markets and towns to the hidden beauties, Costa Rica offers something for everyone.

When organizing your vacation, remember to bring your spirit of adventure, and be prepared to explore. Costa

Rica is full of hidden jewels and unique experiences, so take the time to explore and discover all that it has to offer.

Costa Rica is an extraordinary place that will leave you with memories that will last a lifetime. Whether you're searching for a calm beach holiday or an adventure-filled tour, Costa Rica provides something for everyone. It is a nation rich in beauty, culture, and adventure, and it is guaranteed to make your visit one to remember. So pack your luggage, and get ready to enjoy the beauty and adventure of Costa Rica!

Printed in Great Britain
by Amazon

18120228R00023